HOW TO START A LIP GLOSS BUSINESS

GET YOUR LIP GLOSS COMPANY TO GROW TO THE INTERNATIONAL LEVEL AND EXCEL IN THE LONG-TERM

By

Maxwell Rotheray

Copyright

All rights reserved. No part of this publication **How to Start a Lip Gloss Business** may be reproduced, stored in a retrieval system or transmitted in any form or by any means - electronic, mechanical, photocopying, recording, and scanning without permission in writing by the author.

Table of Contents

Copyright 3

Introduction 7

CHAPTER ONE: How to prepare for success 11

CHAPTER TWO: Branding your Lip Gloss Business 17

CHAPTER THREE: Licensing your Lip Gloss Business 21

CHAPTER FOUR: Cost of starting a new Lip Gloss Business 27

    Starting from the scratch 28

    The cost of lip gloss starting kits 29

    The cost of producing lip gloss 29

CHAPTER FIVE: The profit margin of a successful lip gloss business 33

CHAPTER SIX: How to raise funds for your lip gloss business 35

CHAPTER SEVEN: Finding the right location/customer base 41

    Running the business online 42

    Getting a storefront 44

CHAPTER EIGHT: Business plan for successful lip gloss business 47

    The structure of a typical business plan 49

Business structure 51

CHAPTER NINE: Making the right connections for your lip gloss business 55

CHAPTER TEN: Creating a winning team for your lip gloss business 61

CHAPTER ELEVEN: Preparing for a successful opening day... 67

CHAPTER TWELVE: How to market your business for long-term success 75

CHAPTER THIRTEEN: Steps to scale in the shortest time possible 81

CHAPTER FOURTEEN: How to use technology to boost your sales 85

   Better marketing strategy 86

   Increase productivity 88

   Better transactions and inventory.................. 89

CHAPTER FIFTEEN: Mistakes to avoid when starting a lip gloss business................................. 93

Conclusion 103

Other Books by the Same Author 105

Introduction

As little as they may look, lip glosses are very important to the finishing of make-up. Whether it is used to top a lipstick or just moisturize the natural lips, it makes a lot of difference to almost every age.

I do not think that there will come a time when lip gloss will stop selling. So, I guess you see why you should get into the beauty industry as fast as possible.

There are quite some requirements for the lip gloss business, and for you to succeed, you need to follow them accordingly. Here a step-by-step guide to a successful lip gloss business.

Learning Guideline

1. How to prepare for success
2. Branding your Lip Gloss Business
3. Licensing your Lip Gloss Business
4. Cost of starting a new Lip Gloss Business
   4.1 Starting from the scratch
   4.2 The cost of producing lip gloss

5. The profit margin of a successful lip gloss business
6. How to raise funds for your lip gloss business
7. Finding the right location/customer base
   7.1 Running the business online
   7.2 Getting a storefront
8. Business plan for successful lip gloss business
   8.1 The structure of a typical business plan
9. Making the right connections for your lip gloss business
10. Creating a winning team for your lip gloss business
11. Preparing for a successful opening day
12. How to market your business for long-term success
13. Steps to scale in the shortest time possible
14. How to boost your sales with technology
    14.1 Better marketing strategy
    14.2 Increase productivity

14.3 Better transactions and inventory
15. Mistakes to avoid when starting a lip gloss business
16. Conclusion

CHAPTER ONE: How to prepare for success

How to prepare for success

1. Understand why you want to go into the lip gloss line

People say do what you love, but does this work all the time? I believe that you have a better chance of success if you do what you are good at. Starting a new business line is a serious thing, and you should know precisely why you are getting into it.

Are you in search of a little side business to do, or do you want to make a career out of the lip gloss business? Your purpose will help you to choose how to approach the business.

2. Will you be selling other brands or manufacturing yours?

In as much as both are very fulfilling, they entail different procedures, and you must be ready to fulfill their requirements.

You can make good money from buying readymade lip gloss from big manufacturers to retail. This is a good idea for people who do not want to stay in the lip gloss line for a long time. The startup capital is not intensive, and you will not have anything to lose when you want to drop out of the business.

The potential manufacturers, on the other hand, have to be careful when making their decisions. Though producing the lip gloss itself is not capital intensive, buying the equipment and getting through the branding and licensing process is.

However, it can become much more profitable than just retailing from other producers in the long run.

3. Wholesale or retail; which will you go for?

There are many factors to consider when choosing the scale of business to do. Firstly, it depends on your capital and plan for the company.

You can be a vendor of a brand of lip gloss. Here, you will get a deal with the manufacturers, and they will send you their products in bulk for you to distribute.

But if you are starting your brand, you can do it on a large scale and sell them to distributors. You can also produce them on a medium scale and sell them in retail. As I said, it all depends on you and your finances.

4. Get professional training

If you just want to go into the sales of the finish products, you need to learn some things about makeups and how well they can be applied. Your customers will come seeking answers from you; you are their only link to the manufacturers. So, it is sensible to go through some basic makeup courses and beauty therapy education.

If you are going to become a manufacturer, you need even more professional training. Aim to understand the composition of lip glosses and their various types. How can you produce stable and consistent lip gloss that the public will highly appreciate?

Also, know that you need to understand the safety of the ingredients of your lip gloss. There is no wisdom in spending a considerable sum on producing lip glosses that will irritate the population.

Also, seek to know how to use the equipment effectively for a consistent result. You will also need to learn some necessary business gimmicks if you do not have a strong foundation in business.

There is much work involved in building a good brand and reputation. You may want to learn how other popular brands did theirs and follow their steps.

5. Get a business plan

It's time to get ready for business. Before you go out buying the equipment and raw materials to produce your lip gloss, get a business plan.

Getting a business plan is a very tedious work, and you may never know how to write the most suitable one for your business until you start. But it is essential for the success of your enterprise.

I will be discussing more on the business plan for a lip gloss company in a subsequent section. Hang in there.

6. Understand the trend

People who are crazy about trends will find it a bit easier to succeed in the lip gloss line. Trends for cosmetic product and beauty treatments keep changing, and you have to be always on point with the trends; flow with it.

You can get this by signing up for beauty magazines or blogs and getting their emails per time. Also, you will need to join a group of others in the same business to learn and know how to improve your products without stress.

7. Register your company

Get a permit to sell if you want to become a vendor of cosmetic products. The procedures for obtaining that differ based on the country, state and region. So, know what is required in your locality and follow suit.

As a producer, you will need to get a company name and register. What will you like your brand to be called? Think of it, register, and get the license for your products.

CHAPTER TWO: Branding your Lip Gloss Business

Branding your Lip Gloss Business

Good branding attracts people to a product, and you should be very careful when branding your goods. For lip gloss, branding has a lot to do with the business name, colors for the packaging, and the perfect logo. Let's see how to create a killer brand.

a) Get an attractive business name

The name you pick for your products should not be too complex or difficult to spell or pronounce. Instead, it should be attractive, unique and impossible to forget. There are a lot of lip gloss brands out there, and choosing the right name for yours should not be confusing.

Look up to sites like Wix name generator, Namelix, and the likes to help you choose the right business name.

b) Choose the perfect set of colors for your label

How you design your labels is up to you, but ensure that it is beautiful and easy to read. You will need a graphic designer to help you create the design you have at heart.

However, go for feminine colors like peach, pink and the rest, since women mostly wear lip gloss.

You can also buy brand labels from Etsy. The prices range from $18.

c) Get a professional logo

Design your logo if you can, or hire a professional designer to make one for you. To have a good idea of the kind of logo you need, look at the other lip gloss brands or samples on the internet.

There are experts on freelance sites like Upwork and Fiverr that create unique logos for a token.

CHAPTER THREE: Licensing your Lip Gloss Business

Licensing your Lip Gloss Business

Lip gloss falls under 'defined cosmetics' by FDA; so, you must get their approval before going on with your business. There are various requirements before getting this license, and they are summarized below.

1. The product must not be misbranded or adulterated

The FDA is against the production of adulterated cosmetics and prohibits their use. It considers a lip gloss and other cosmetics to be adulterated if it contains substances that are harmful to the body when used according to its customary purpose.

This means that if you produce your lip gloss with putrid, filthy, or decomposed substance or in an unclean environment, it is not fit for license or sales.

There is also a rule governing the type of coloring that must be used. Although there are exemptions for some irritable colorings, not everyone is in the group. Find out the most suitable and permitted colorings to use before producing your lip gloss.

Also, your product needs to have the right labeling and information on ingredient. It must not be misleading or carry wrong information about the substance in the container. If you do this, then to the FDA, your product is misleading, and you will not be granted a license.

2. Cosmetic labeling

If your lip gloss will be distributed in the United States, then your labeling must company with the regulations as published by the FDA under the FD&C and FP&L act.

The 'labeling' here refers to the label and every other graphics or printed out materials accompanying the product. According to the FD&C, the labeling and statement of the net content of the ingredients must be present both inside and outside the container or wrapper of the product.

"The information panel must carry the name and address of the company producing it. The principal display panel (the part of the label that will be most likely displayed on the product) must carry the illustration and descriptive name, use of the product, a correct statement of the content of the lip gloss (measure, weight, and numerical count)."

3. Declaration of ingredient

You are demanded to make the information on the ingredients you use for the lip gloss conspicuous to be easily read during purchase. Also, you must list out the ingredients in order of descending predominance. All this label information must be written in English in a manner that customers can easily understand.

4. Label warnings

Before submitting your product for licensing by the FDA, test it for safety. If you do not carry out a substantial test for its safety, the product will be considered misbranded, attracting regulatory actions. But you can avoid this action by stating a warning on the label that the safety of the product has not been tested.

5. Law enforcement authority

Getting a license for your lip gloss business is vital, and failure to do so is punishable by law. This law governs both the products produced in the country and those imported. Many people have had the FDA launch a criminal action against them for committing the same offence.

CHAPTER FOUR: Cost of starting a new Lip Gloss Business

Cost of starting a new Lip Gloss Business

The cost of starting a lip gloss business depends on how you want to do it. You can choose to sell popular lip gloss brands, work with private label suppliers of lip gloss, or start yours from scratch. But let us look at the cost implication of starting from scratch.

Starting from the scratch

Like every business, you need to count your cost before getting in. The price of starting a lip gloss business is based on three aspects:

- The cost of product development
- Marketing
- Business expenses

People mostly consider the cost of product development when starting a business. It has to do with the amount required to get the raw materials, develop the product and get it to the end-user.

Aside from this, you should take into consideration the cost of blending and mixing the ingredients, and packaging the finished products. However, this will not make much sense if you do not have the starting kits for producing lip gloss.

The cost of lip gloss starting kits

There are available starting kits for your lip gloss business that fits any budget. In them, you will find a few hundred units of ingredient stickers, tubes, and private label lip gloss. You can also get some with a box and logo design. The cost of basic kits is $1000.

The cost of producing lip gloss

There are many lip gloss producing techniques, and you can find many of them for free online. But you practicalize first with them before taking them to the market.

The cost of producing these lip glosses will depend on the type and formulation you are going for. Of course, the basic lip gloss formulation will not cost the same as the glitter and metallic formulas and the other exquisite ones.

It costs between $0.10 and $3 to produce a pound of lip gloss, but the average is $1. It should also take you $1 per unit to package and label the product as well. So, you can just plan to use $2 to $3 to produce each unit of lip gloss. This, however, the exact cost of production depends on the size of each unit.

- **Large scale production of lip gloss**

When approaching lip gloss production on a large scale, you will leverage the economy of scales to have a lower production cost and higher profit. The price of producing a unit of lip gloss for $2 - $3 is only possible if you are making 500 to 1,000 units. But if you are targeting anything lesser, your cost of production will be higher, and this will influence the price of your finished product and maybe your profit margin.

- **Medium-scale lip gloss production**

It can be capital intensive to start up a medium scale lip gloss business. More money will be spent on getting a facility for the production and buying equipment for mixing, blending, and packaging the products.

Aside from this, you should not spend much on buying the raw materials, servicing the truck for distribution, producing the actual product, paying utility bills, and paying your employees.

CHAPTER FIVE: The Profit Margin of a Successful Lip Gloss Business

The Profit Margin of a Successful Lip Gloss Business

In 2019, the total sales of lip gloss were approximately $126.54 million. That is a whole lot of money and lip gloss. But these figures don't come easy. It depends on the amount of lip gloss you produce and sell.

The sales of lip gloss depend mostly on the trend and timing. Lip gloss sells more in some seasons than others, and you need to know how to target your market.

But despite this, the profit margin you will get from your lip gloss business is dependent on two factors:

- The revenue generated from the lip gloss sales
- The cost of production.

So, if you want to know how much you have gained, subtract the total amount of money in your account after selling out your lip gloss by the amount it cost you to produce them (if you started from scratch) or buy them (if you are just a vendor).

CHAPTER SIX: How to Raise Funds for Your Lip Gloss Business

How to Raise Funds for Your Lip Gloss Business

It can feel like there is an eternal quest for money when starting a new lip gloss business, especially on a large scale. Except you spent your life working for the funds to start a business, you will need some help raising funds.

Here are some ways you can find funds for your lip gloss business:

1. Crowdfunding

Crowdfunding allows you to meet people in your thinking class. You can check out how much your business will interest people and pitch to influential personalities with the network, but that is not all. It also helps you meet people who are willing to support your business and launch funding campaigns for it.

Many sites offer these services, but most of them work the same way. You need to pitch, telling people why your product is essential, the problem it solves and who you need the support from. You will have better chances if you run a good website and PR.

You need to join sites like Fundable, Indiegogo, Fundly, etc., to raise funds with crowdfunding.

2. Personal finance

Let us face the fact; people will hardly invest in a business that the owner has not invested anything. It is risky to start a business, investors know this, and it is even one reason new businesses find it challenging to get traditional loans.

You can invest your savings if you have any or sell out your home if considering a second mortgage is not outrageous.

3. Venture capitalists

Unlike traditional bank loans, venture capitalists prefer to invest in upcoming businesses with great potentials for success and tangible returns. But this is not all.

Venture capitalists also seek to have some part of the equity in return for their investment and a voice in the company's affairs. Since venture capitalists are making money off their investment, they feel it is necessary to have some control over the company's management.

4. Angel investors

Angel investors are worth over a million dollars or have their yearly income higher than $200,000. They are always looking for upcoming promising businesses to invest in exchange for a share of the equity. They can support solitarily or as a group.

Before getting funds from an angel investor, you must have a good business plan and pitch. Also, the investor and investment must be registered with the Securities and Exchange Commission (SEC).

5. Family members

It can be pretty easy to raise funds from friends and family members that believe in you. Though this is not the best idea for some, you can get tangible help if you know how to narrow down your list and approach genuinely interested people.

When you find an interested person, make formal agreements on the form the money is taking (whether it is a loan or exchange for equity). If it is a loan, you can seal the agreement by using a peer to peer website to document.

6. Loans

Getting a loan is another good idea for raising money if you are sure that your business will go as planned. There many loan options ranging from your credit card, traditional loans, and microloans.

Many small scale entrepreneurs do not usually qualify for the traditional loan, so they rely on the microloan. Though microloans were primarily developed for non-profits, they still extend their benevolence to entrepreneurs that do not qualify for the traditional loan.

CHAPTER SEVEN: Finding The Right Location/Customer Base

Finding The Right Location/Customer Base

Firstly, you fix your mind on where you want to run your lip gloss business. Some people prefer to take it online and have an online-only shop or one that compliments the physically located one.

Running the business online

It is pretty easy to get established online. There are different platforms, and all of them work well.

- **Get your website**

You can get a website for your business online. Options like Wix, Shopify, and Squarespace makes it easy for you to set up an online store without much cost. However, ensure that you use your social media accounts to promote the products on your website by mentioning links on them.

- **The social media**

A major part of world's population is on social media like Facebook, Twitter, and Instagram. Many people have also succeeded in building a good customer base for their businesses on Facebook and Instagram. There are many marketing tools to help you advertise and take your business to the right audience.

Of course, young and middle-aged people are most concerned about lip gloss, and you must know how to target them. Place ads and do not hesitate to pay a token to promote them if need be.

Your location matters. Ensure that your ads are not displaying to people in Australia when you are in the U.S., except you are willing to ship just one or two pieces of lip gloss that way.

- **Established stores like Etsy and Amazon**

If you need a platform with an already established customer base, sell on platforms like Etsy and Amazon. These platforms have millions of people selling and buying from them, and it should not be difficult to meet customers interested in your product.

Etsy even helps new sellers promote their products for free during their first few weeks to help them get the customer base. You can start here while waiting to get the desired amount of traffic for your website.

Getting a storefront

It is cheaper to sell online than a physical store, but aside from the cost, there are other advantages of a physical store. However, when choosing the location for your physical store, consider the following:

- **Demographics:** What does your local area look like? You need to locate your business close to your target audience.
- **The set-up cost:** As a make-up shop that your business is, you need to consider the cost of setting up the decoration and display. The colors should be catchy to the feminine nature, and your placement should attract even an onlooker.
- **Competition:** It is crucial to consider the other businesses that are situated close to yours. What are they selling? Do they have an already established customer base for lip gloss? If they do, how do you intend

to stand out? If there is an already existing lip gloss or makeup shop, ensure you have a unique selling point that will draw the customers to yourself.

If you do not have plans to sell your products wholesale, it can be pretty awkward to open a brick and mortar store. You can attach to your lip gloss business the sales of other products to attract customers.

- **Foot traffic:** Small businesses can thrive exceptionally in an area with good foot traffic. Your business should be sited at a place where people quickly move and get crowded. You do not want your lip gloss being stocked up in the store without anyone stopping by, even to say hi.

When going for a brick and mortar store, always consider the need for an online one to back it up. It will help with the advertisement of the store and improve your sales. Who knows? It may be your only means of meeting a wider audience.

CHAPTER EIGHT: Business Plan for Successful Lip Gloss Business

Business Plan for Successful Lip Gloss Business

Writing a business plan for your business is the first thing you should consider before starting the business. It is what determines the path and success of your business. Writing the best business plan for your business does not come easy.

However, to write a good business plan, you need to do your feasibility studies and market research to know if it is even possible for the business to succeed in your environment.

From the results you gathered during the market research, find answers to the following questions:

- What are the types of lip gloss you want to sell or produce?
- What do you need to start up the business?
- What marketing strategies will you use for your lip gloss business?
- Who are the highest-ranking competitors, and what are their

marketing strategies? How do you plan to top the competition?
- Will you secure a wholesale distribution or an eCommerce site?
- Who will take care of the administration?

The structure of a typical business plan

Here is a template on how you should arrange your business plan.

1. **Industry overview**

This segment is for you to write out the general facts about the industry, its history and statistics of companies in the business. It should also include the usefulness of the product and why it is recommended for use.

Are their challenges facing the lip gloss industry? Do well to state them in this segment, as it will guide you on how to overcome them when you get into the business?

Also, state the profitability of the business and if it is sensible for small scale or large scale entrepreneurs to undertake.

2. Executive summary

This is everything about your company; it should tell who you are and what you produce. Are you just a company for the production of lip gloss, or are other products attached?

This segment should be similar to the "about us" page on your website, and it should be written in detail so that it can paint a good picture for a visitor that has never heard anything about your brand.

Feel free to brag (responsibly) about the brand (or one you would like to create). It is believed that if you have a good view of your company at heart, you will be guided appropriately to creating one that is highly admired by customers.

3. Products and services

Though you roughly mentioned the products and services you offer in the segment above, it is time to list them in details. You will need to include the license you have and the areas you will be selling your products.

4. **Mission and vision statement**

This is where you write out your vision and mission statement.

Business structure

This segment has to do with the administrative aspect of your business. What skill do you need from the people you hire?

An everyday lip gloss business should have a chief executive officer (CEO), plant manager, human resources and admin manager, merchandize manager, sales and marketing manager, machine operators, accountants/cashiers, and distribution truck drivers.

5. **Job roles and responsibilities**

Here you will list out the details of the responsibility for each position. You may need to look into the professional duties of these positions and how they apply to your workplace.

6. **SWOT analysis**

SWOT stands for strength, weaknesses, opportunities, and threats. It takes an earnest analysis of your company's strengths and weakness. It could be attitudinal, financial, or otherwise. The opportunities you have are the advantage you have over the other companies in the industry, and the threats are those downturns that may affect your progress in the industry.

7. **Market analysis**

This has to do with your understanding of the current developments in the industry. The trends in production, style, and packaging, and also in the safety of the materials used in the production of lip gloss.

If the ones in the market are not so safe, you can opt for lip gloss with fewer chemicals than the available ones.

8. **Target market**

This involves the groups of people that will mainly use your products. Yes, the product can be for everyone, but there is a set that will buy them wholesale.

9. **Sales and marketing strategy**

This has to do with everything from where you intend to get your source of income to how you intend to take the goods to the public. You should also write out in details the marketing strategy you want to employ.

You should also include your sales forecast for the first three fiscal years and your strategies for publicizing and advertising.

10. Pricing strategy

Pricing is very important to the sales of your cosmetics. Will you like to start selling your products at a lower price first during the first few months before normalizing the price? Whatever your choice may be ensure you do not end up demeaning your product when compared to others.

It is also safe to include your payment options, especially if you will have an online shop. And most importantly, ensure that the options you include are in concordance with US financial rules and regulations.

11. Budget for startup

Here, you need to list the detailed estimate of the amount you will spend to start up the lip gloss business from scratch (if that is what you are doing). You should also create a segment that states where you will be getting the income to startup.

12. Strategy for sustainability and expansion

Every successful business must grow, and this does not just happen. It takes a proper plan and development of timely milestones to ensure that a company grows at the pace you want.

About sustainability, you will need to write out a rock-solid statement on how you intend to share the profit. In addition to that, create a checklist that will help you know the pace you are growing, the goals you have achieved and the ones you have not.

If you have issues writing out a good business plan for your business alone, contact a knowledgeable friend or professional to help you out. The success of your business plan plays a very vital role in the success of your business.

CHAPTER NINE: Making The Right Connections for Your Lip Gloss Business

Making The Right Connections for Your Lip Gloss Business

Every successful small scale entrepreneur benefits invariably from a connection of professionals. Ranging from solutions to problems and recommendations to increase sales, the help of a network of professionals cannot be easily overlooked.

That is why you need to follow this guide to know how to get yourself the best connections.

1. **Acknowledge that you need help**

Keeping in mind that you need more answers and ideas in getting the job done will always keep you on the lookout for possible solutions.

Also, you can start learning the art of curiosity that will push you to speak up when the time is right.

2. **Know what your challenges are and be serious about finding a solution**

Knowing the exact thing you need to make the business more successful will allow you to narrow your search for connections to the right people. Also, you can tell your team about the challenge of the business and get them to find answers and make connections for the company.

3. Find a way you can be of help to others

Now that you know the kind of connections you need to build, it is good you find a way of being relevant to the people you meet.

A lot of people make the mistake of immediately dumping all their questions and needs on their connections right on the go. This is not just wrong; it is parasitic.

To have a connection that has the potential of lasting in the long term, offer something useful to your relationship. It is even better if you make the first move to give. This way, they will feel more relaxed and willing to reciprocate.

4. Provide solutions on social media

Many people will want to reach out to you when they see what you are doing. Some will come to build a link and do business with you, while others may come for help. This way, you can select the kind of people relevant to your company without jumping from pillar to post to find them.

You can build this kind of audience by providing your industry-relevant contents to your followers on Twitter, LinkedIn, and Facebook.

5. Go out to where you can meet new people

Go out to places where people in your industry will likely gather. Go to fares and exhibitions, even mix up with people in your neighborhood; you never know where you will meet your luck.

Besides going to gatherings related to your field, you can also visit those of other areas and industry. You may get a new idea or find a person that is willing to collaborate.

6. Get your colleagues to know each other

When you have made the needed connection, create events that will bring your colleagues together. When they get to know themselves, they will start a conversation that will lead to even better innovations.

CHAPTER TEN: Creating A Winning Team for Your Lip Gloss Business

Creating A Winning Team for Your Lip Gloss Business

To succeed in your lip gloss business, you need to work with people; possibly form a team. If you do not get them now, you will need them as your business grows. The first thing you need is to know the people you need in your team and how to fetch them. Put the requirements you need together and select the most suitable people.

When you do, follow this guide to make for yourself a winning team.

1. Create a clear vision

The business is yours, and your team is there to help you achieve the goal. You need to have something on the ground for them to follow. If it is a shared project, and you want to build a partnership, make plans together and decide on the final aim of the company.

But as a team leader, the team expects you to know where you are going and understand (even if not wholly) how to get there. There should also be a means to measure the progress of the team along the way.

Getting this right is usually the challenge of many teams and companies, but you can save yourself and your team from this tragedy if you narrow your priorities to three or less. Deciding what these three goals are will be your most significant task as a team leader because everyone's work will flow from the goals. Take your time to line out these plans as the slightest mistake could flip the team all over.

2. Respect their personalities

Your team member will come from different backgrounds and have different personalities; your ability to understand them makes you a great leader. Understand their strengths, weaknesses and emotional languages and address them accordingly.

The personality difference will make some people better at a role than others. For instance, an extrovert will do great at the counter, and a sparky sanguine will kill it in marketing.

3. Allocate duties

There will be lesser clashes and confusion when everyone has clear and distinct roles and set deadlines. You can have some sub-teams if your central team is large enough. Also, remind your team members and sub-groups of their responsibilities even when they are basic and repetitive.

Also, ensure you have a target to measure the success; if not, everyone will have to measure the progress their way and end up in inseparable fights and arguments.

4. Welcome spontaneity

Every team can benefit significantly from the members' instincts; that is why they were even needed at first. You should expect this from your team. However, you need to set boundaries, but within them, let your team explore and operate on their instincts.

When you allow the introduction of new and somewhat strange (but related) ideas, you will barely have noticeable lapses from the strengths and weakness of the team.

5. Appreciate them

A happy team is a successful team; this lies significantly with how you react to their contributions to the company. Show your team that they are loved and valued, and they will turn your company into a family that others will wish they belonged.

CHAPTER ELEVEN: Preparing for A Successful Opening Day

Preparing for A Successful Opening Day

The success of an opening day has a lot to do with the crowd you draw and the lasting impact you create to make them keep coming back. So, how do you achieve this?

1. Start with your close circle

Like I mentioned earlier, to have a successful opening day, you must have a crowd. Your place will be more inviting if it looks like there are many people there (like staff) doing one thing or the other.

Since you are just starting, it may be challenging to get all that number, so get your close circle; if you have an existing business, take workers from there to fill the space. However, the number you should get should not be outrageous; it should be suitable for your company's size.

Their work will involve organizing, meeting the needs of visitors, or just moving around the place with a warm smile.

2. Promote on social media

The information about your event will be widespread once you and your friends get it on your social media accounts. Use sponsored ads to make them even more popular. This should be done early on so that people can start making their plans to visit.

Using other paid advertising strategies works even better. A good PR will plan a good brand awareness strategy for you and will show you how to maximize your use of email marketing and other forms of targeted campaigns.

With the right connections and advert plans on ground, your opening day will be the talk of the place, and you will host it like a celeb.

3. Invite the media

Getting the media involved with your event paves the way to more success after opening the business. They will help you publicize and get more people to know about the place.

You do not need to go for very expensive or high-class media. Your local media outlets and networking groups work well, if not better. They will take the information right to the people that should patronize you the most.

4. Invite your local dignitaries

Having dignitaries in your opening event will open you up to better opportunities in the future alongside the sales you will enjoy on that day.

Start with the dignitaries in your local area like the business leaders, mayor, city council member, etc.

5. Give it a professional setting

We cannot overemphasis the need for giving your company a perfect professional outlook. To achieve this, take care of your branding. Starting from the logo to an attractive company name, product branding (which must have been done already), and even a branded T-shirt (or whatever it is you will be wearing on that day).

6. Create freebies

People go back to the places that offered them free stuff. Even if they do not like you, giving them high-quality, unique freebies will make them think of you specially and attach a level of respect.

Let this freebie be a way of telling the whole world 'hello, I only offer quality here', and they will look up to you for whatever needs they have in that area. It could help you build the real-time connections you need. And lest I forget, attach your contact to the freebie. If they are not willing to take your company fliers around and on social media, your freebies will announce you wherever they take them.

7. Staff effectively

Besides just getting your staff and close circle to help you fill the place and do the job, you need to train them to approach your visitors. Let them know how well they can support and make your customers comfortable during the event.

These visitors will be your first customers, and how you treat those sets the tone for your enterprise. If you treat them well, they will leave good reviews for you on your website and flag off your company well.

8. Have a contingency plan

When opening your business, one of the ways of avoiding failure is by expecting it. Something may go wrong, by the way; you just need to be prepared enough to handle it.

Get your team ready and on standby to fix anything that may go wrong. They should be capable; it may be a major fault or minor mishap. A friend of mine was opening his business, and something went wrong with the wiring. Who would have thought of that?

For you, it may be something like a very long queue; get prepared for anything.

9. Talking about very long queues, prepare for more

People underestimate the impact of their business and get overwhelmed when they get better responses. And as a starter, you may be so concerned about getting the customers to come without realizing that there may be more willing people than you think.

Are you ready to handle partners? What of selling your products to people in locations that are far from where you are?

It is better to be over-prepared. Learn both the cost and procedures of shipping and managing large crowds. It will be terrible to turn away potential loyal customers because you were underprepared.

10. Create more awareness with prints

There are many ideas for promoting a business with prints. Let your marketing expert tell you how well to use prints to promote your business and market your brand.

The use of business cards, flyers, signs, banners, brochures, and course invitations are essential to your promotions, and you need to know how to use them.

11. Get contact information

There are customers that you may never see again if you do not get a hold of them on the first day. You may never know those customers, so it is safer to get their contacts and email when they are there.

While this sounds easy, you should offer them something in exchange for their sign up; you do not want to be a burden to them. It could be anything; a point on your loyalty program, a percentage off for their next purchase, or even the chance of winning a gift card.

12. Offer rewards for next visits

You will likely have customers that will buy something on the first day, but getting them to come back is usually the problem for many people. It should not be for you.

A customer will likely come back when you offer them a reward on their next visit. It could be a discount or coupon, but try not to give too much away. Having your customers come back again is a significant factor for success.

CHAPTER TWELVE: How to Market Your Business for Long-Term Success

How to Market Your Business for Long-Term Success

Setting up your business is one thing, and getting to stand the test of time is another. Many lip gloss businesses spring up now and then, but not all of them last longer than a year. Here is how to get your lip gloss company to grow to the international level and excel in the long term.

- **Have a long term strategy**

There is no way you can be a part of the future when you have not planned for it. Consider your business and the most suitable expansion project you will have for it. Take some time to study the market and how it is shifting, and try predicting the direction it is moving.

With this in mind, set some vital goals and break them into achievable units. Tell your team and ensure you put it into writing. This should even be a part of your business plan. Work towards this plan and let it guide every step you take.

- **Be flexible**

In as much as a long term plan is good, when not handled with flexibility, it can be the root cause of your enterprise's failure. The market is currently changing, and some campaigns may work while others can make you fall flat on your face.

The principal goal of the company should remain, but keep yourself, team, and company structure open to some adjustments that may be necessary during the journey. Also, carefully consider how every step and change of plan will aid or break the company.

- **Have strong connections**

Aside from your team, you need to connect well with good suppliers, HRs, and other business partners with all respect to the law. But when you have a long term vision, ensure that the partners you have share the same core values as the company.

Partnering with an already established company in your target market will give you an edge in your sales as customers will see you as a more credible producer.

It may be challenging to decide the partnership that will be valuable in the future when you are just resuming. So, do your part by being reliable with your partners until they prove to be undeserving.

- **Be relevant**

There is severe competition in the lip gloss market, and you need to know how to stand out. Do not forget that there are brands that have already made a niche for themselves and have part of the market. Choose your place wisely and know where to fill it.

There should be something that makes your products stand out from the regular lip gloss customers to use every day. Do something that makes your lip gloss unique and be known for that. If there is nothing new you can do, offer excellent customer service, be kind and reliable, and people will keep coming back to you.

- **Use the right marketing strategies**

There are different marketing strategies, and picking the right one or combination will make all the difference. These marketing strategies should help your company to craft quality advertisement and send them out through the right channels.

The following are the marketing strategies you can use:

- Branding
- Content marketing
- Radio
- Search Engine Optimization
- Social media

Committing yourself to these keys will help you have a long term marketing strategy.

- **Examine and adjust your business structure**

As you grow in the business, you will understand the industry more and notice the company structure you need to adjust. Hence, it is important to make your internal systems adjustable since it influences your business's efficiency.

- **Consistently communicate with your target audience**

To boost your ROI, you need to create a long term marketing strategy. This has a lot to do with consistency and frequency. Alongside the frequency and consistency, build awareness with your target audience. Keep your audience posted about your new developments to help them feel familiar with the business.

CHAPTER THIRTEEN: Steps to Scale in The Shortest Time Possible

Steps to Scale in The Shortest Time Possible

It is believed that it can take up to 2 or 3 years for a small scale business to be well established and successful. However, this duration will not be possible if you do not do the business clean. What do I mean by this?

1. Do what you've got to do

On the surface, it may feel like it is easier to do the job shabbily and jump into starting your lip gloss line. But read my lips; shabby jobs don't land anyone in success.

Take your time to do the business plan and market survey, register the company, brand and license your products like a pro, and step into business, knowing that the most important things have been settled. Then get running!

2. Be wise with your finances

Many people spend too much at the start of the business and then are left with nothing in the middle. Companies do not pay off immediately, so you will still need to invest down the line.

3. Build a good team

Don't just hire people because you have a personal relationship with them. Do so because they have the character and skill needed for the success of your company. If your team is lacking in some way, train them.

4. Market madly

You can have thousands of lip gloss units still sitting in your warehouse after putting your best into the business. Marketing is your way of taking what you have got to the world; do with all enthusiasm. However, be sure that your products are worth the hype.

5. Have a good customer service

Most customers contribute reasonable to the business, and many will not return if you do not treat them well. Every customer is important; treat them accordingly.

6. Give room for the unexpected

Your target audience might turn out to like something different from what you have got.

Do not give up on them. Follow them up, find what they need and feed them with it.

CHAPTER FOURTEEN: How to Use Technology to Boost Your Sales

How to Use Technology to Boost Your Sales

Thinking of using technology to boost your sales can be overwhelming at first, but trust me, there is nothing complicated there. It has proven itself to be highly useful whether your business is technology-related or not. Lip gloss has nothing to do with technology, but the appropriate use of technology can be the game-changer. Let me show you how.

Better marketing strategy
- **The social media**

The first time my grandma started accepting social media was when I helped her sell some of her embroidered pieces on Instagram. The effectiveness of social media in expanding your customer reach is almost magical.

But aside from this, using social media to promote your business helps you build better relationships with your customer. They will feel like they can connect with you on a personal level. You can quickly drop the freebie that brings everyone to your page before feeding them with the real thing you have to offer.

From here, you will be open to getting private feedback on your products and suggestions on how to make them better.

- **Web and mobile platform**

In today's world, websites have become a necessity for a successful business. Customers prefer to go online and read reviews about a company or product, and if you are outstanding at what you do, it can be an excellent place to show off your praises.

Optimize your website for mobile. You know that 80% of searches and online transactions are done from mobile devices, and you do not want to be left out. And since people prefer to window shop online before getting the real thing at physical shops, you can add a cart to help them buy your product from the comfort of their homes. Then you can devise means to get the goods shipped directly to their doorstep.

- **Free Wi-Fi**

Do you ever wonder why people never stop going to the coffee shop? The free Wi-Fi! People are compelled to buy some coffee even when they do not need it and keep returning to the same shop.

You can also employ this strategy. Start by making your physical store compatible with internet users. They will stay for a long time. But since you will be opening a lip gloss shop (which may not be compatible with staying for a long time), enable Wi-Fi to keep them coming back.

They will buy from you and even share your business on their social media page, getting more friends interested. I see this as a one-off opportunity to widen your reach.

Increase productivity

Introducing technology to your business will improve your productivity and efficiency. It will also help you carry out some work instead of employing another helping hand.

For instance, getting more advanced equipment for production and packaging will help quicken your time spent and the number of units you produce a day. It will also decrease your manual energy and the cost of production.

Better transactions and inventory

- **Square**

When starting up a small business, it is common to do the cash-only form of payment, but this is archaic; it is stressful to follow through—adding a piece of technology like Square (a card reader that you will plug into your phone or tablet).

You will benefit from the free and easy to use Point of Sales software app that it has. You can use your mobile device to process payment or even set it up on a countertop. It is smaller and less-space consuming than the traditional POS system.

This will help you process your payment faster and have enough extra time to deal with other things. It will also save you from losing customers; most of them no longer carry cash.

- **Introduce an app or card system**

A customer will prefer to buy the same product from another producer with money-saving technology. It could be an app that gives deals and coupons or a gift card system. I understand that this comes with its own initial cost, but it is usually worth it in the long run.

Customers tend to buy more if they feel they are saving money; they do not even mind spending more money. Also, they appreciate it more when you give them exclusive membership cards. They will feel special and commit themselves more to your company. For you, this means them coming back time and time again for more sales.

- **Enable mobile payment**

Enabling online payment for people buying online, subscribing online or renewing their membership makes it easy for them to carry out more spontaneous purchase. This will help you receive more prompt payments and wave bye to bounced checks that come with the billing or invoicing system.

- **More knowledgeable employees**

Employees will find it easier to take inventory of the stock when you have everything laid out and accessible from a mobile device. You will have no challenge in trusting them because everything that leaves the shop will be quickly and adequately documented.

Also, research even proved that 20% of customers even use their mobile phones to make enquiries about some information and available goods because they believe it will be faster and accurate.

CHAPTER FIFTEEN: Mistakes to Avoid When Starting a Lip Gloss Business

Mistakes to Avoid When Starting a Lip Gloss Business

Many things can go wrong with your lip gloss business when you do not do your homework. This is a list of common mistakes entrepreneurs make and how you can avoid them.

1. **Having an inadequate business plan**

I have discussed the importance of having a business plan, but it is not enough to have one. How detailed is your plan? Does it have all the essential aspects of your future business clearly stated?

Included in it should be your long and short term goals, sources of finance, market research and even details about your marketing strategy.

2. **Not having a sure source of income**

Do not even think that you will start feeding off the business right from inception. It does not work that way. And how will you even kick start the business when there is no specific amount of money on ground?

People start with a bank loan while others kick off with their savings. You can get sponsors if your business plan is outstanding. Whatever it may be, ensure you have a reliable income source that will take you to run the design and startup until the business starts bringing in substantial profit.

3. Lacking a comprehensive understanding of your business

Helena Rubinstein became rich selling beauty, you too can, but this lies in understanding your purpose of creating new lip gloss. The world will not applaud you for creating a money stream for yourself; it will for your passion for making humanity better. How does your lip gloss better society?

Your sure step to success is developing a product that solves a problem; it is what will set you apart from the other numerous lip gloss brands in the world. This means having a unique selling proposition.

Besides knowing this unique selling proposition, you should also know how to communicate it to the world. I can walk off the healthiest and delicious meal if the chef does not know how to express his thoughts to me. It is the same with beauty products and women. Have your strength and communicate it directly to the hearts of women.

4. Improper branding

This is related to the previous. The world may never know the value of what you have developed except you tell it to them. How do you do this? Through good branding.

A gap in your branding can portray a different image of your products and intentions to your customers. Save yourself the hassle and take every little aspect of branding seriously.

Go for a professional logo, and choose the most suitable colors and image for your company. It may cost a bit, but it is one of your most essential chances to stand out of the crowd.

5. Not having a professional accountant

You need to create a separate bank account for your business. The line between the family's money and business' money is a crucial one, and you do not want to risk a mix-up. With this, you will tell your initial investments and know-how to set the business so you do not lose out.

Besides getting a separate account for your business, you need a professional accountant to manage your finance. There is a lot of financial work to do, and adding it with the production and other parts of the business is setting yourself up for failure because you cannot do it all alone. Get help!

6. Inadequate market research

Maybe it should have made this the second point after the business plan because of its vitality. Many people just jump into the production of lip gloss without taking their time to study the market, and at the end of the day, they lose the money and sit up frustrated.

Market research does not only help with giving you leads on how to price your products. The primary aim is to help you know the kind of similar products out there and what people are willing to buy. When this aspect is not done correctly, you can produce goods that are lesser in quality than the ones in the market.

7. Poor self-assessment

Most times, we think that we are perfect for running the kind of business we desire, but not so. Our attitudes, strengths and weaknesses could have an adverse effect on our business and hinder our success.

Is there anything about you that almost everyone complains about? How will it affect your business? If you do not have good interpersonal skills, it is a good idea to avoid the counter (if you are into retail). Hire someone to do it for you. Also, if you are good, smart and outgoing, you can take up your advertising part.

8. Being ignorant of the competition

Like it or not, you will be exposed to a lot of competition in the lip gloss line, and you must be ready to follow it. This means that you need to see what your competitors are doing and find ways to produce what is better.

There is no harm in purchasing their products to see where they are getting it wrong. It's not sneaky; it is just you trying to provide the population with something more satisfying.

Not being able to keep up with this can be detrimental to your business. You may end up producing so much of the same thing and not know when the market moved away from there.

9. Poor marketing

Let's assume you have the best lip gloss idea that should bring the world kneeling at your feet; developing it and keeping the idea to yourself will not make your dreams come true. The world will not come, not even your next-door neighbor.

Marketing is the thin line that draws between successful and unsuccessful business. Even a business without the best ideas sells more than a unique company with an extraordinary idea.

Most times, we complain about the money, and some people even see investing in marketing as a waste. It is not. Do not be tempted to put all your eggs in the basket of free marketing. Though they work, they can take forever before their results become visible.

10. Inadequate online marketing

This is the 21st century, and many people decide on the products they want to buy, read reviews on them and even complete the transactions there. Not having good online marketing is too much of a loss for you as a business person.

You can use any social media platform to promote your business; they include Etsy, Facebook, or LinkedIn. Your sales will go up when many people on the web can see your products and have a direct link to where they can pay for them.

11. Giving out too many discounts

I mentioned giving discounts, coupons, and freebies on your opening day, but overdoing it is not good. Count your cost for offering discount and consider their retail value.

Also, instead of just dashing out your products, go for value-added orders. You can offer free shipping for people who buy up to a certain number of products or add one piece free for every specific number of products they buy. Still, you need to count the cost of the product and your profit margin.

Bigger manufacturers will find this easy because of their reduced production cost, but the small and medium scale may not.

Conclusion

The lip gloss business is very lucrative if you know how well to follow it up. It can be daunting at the start, but it usually turns out to be fun and worthy as time goes on.

Do you want to make lip gloss for profits? Trust the guide in this book.

Other Books by the Same Author

- How to Start a Photography Business: A Beginner's Guide to A Successful Career as A Photographer
- How to Invest in Real Estate (For Beginners): Make Your First $100,000 Using This Powerful Real Estate Business Model
- How to Start A Drop Shipping Business: Make Your First $1,000 Using This Powerful Drop Shipping Business Model
- How to Start a Cleaning Business: Make Your First $100,000 Using This Powerful Commercial Cleaning Business Model

www.ingramcontent.com/pod-product-compliance
Lightning Source LLC
Chambersburg PA
CBHW031439210526
45464CB00005B/2266